AFRICAN-AMERICAN SPIRITUALS

```
— PIANO LEVEL —
EARLY INTERMEDIATE
(HLSPL LEVEL 4-5)
```

ISBN 978-0-634-01721-6

HAL•LEONARD® CORPORATION

7777 W. BLUEMOUND RD. P.O. BOX 13819 MILWAUKEE, WI 53213

Visit Hal Leonard Online at
www.halleonard.com

PREFACE

The rich tunes and powerful lyrics of these spirituals make them a priceless part of America's musical heritage.

"If religion was a thing that money could buy,
the rich would live and the poor would die..."

"Swing low, sweet chariot, comin' for to carry me home..."

These songs are simple, yet profoundly moving. Spirituals come from the period of slavery in America. They communicate the pain of the slave's predicament, and the joy born from a faith in a better life after death.

Spirituals have influenced countless classical and popular composers. Some believe that spirituals are the very foundation for what later became jazz. Jazz musicians turn to them for improvisational foundations. People all around the world find joy and inspiration in them.

"The sun shines bright on the cloudiest day,
oh, rock-a-my soul.
A prayer is all you need to light your way,
oh, rock-a-my soul."

Like the spirituals themselves, these arrangements were written to be easily playable yet full sounding. Play them soulfully!

With best wishes,
Phillip Keveren

BIOGRAPHY

Phillip Keveren, a multi-talented keyboard artist and composer, has composed original works in a variety of genres from piano solo to symphonic orchestra. Mr. Keveren gives frequent concerts and workshops for teachers and their students in the United States, Canada, Europe, and Asia. Mr. Keveren holds a B.M. in composition from California State University Northridge and a M.M. in composition from the University of Southern California.

CONTENTS

ALL MY TRIALS

African-American Spiritual
Arranged by Phillip Keveren

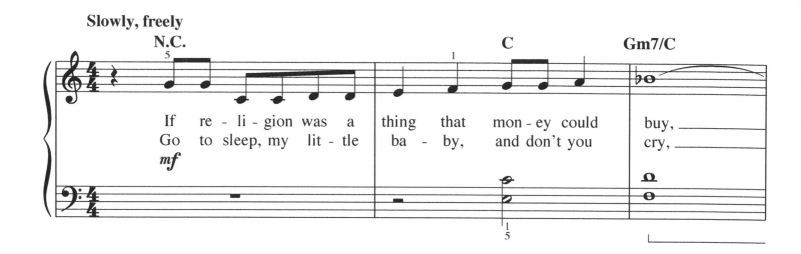

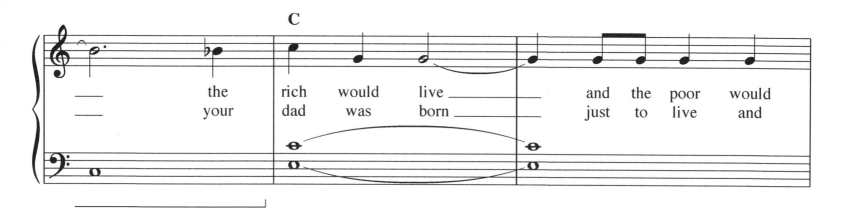

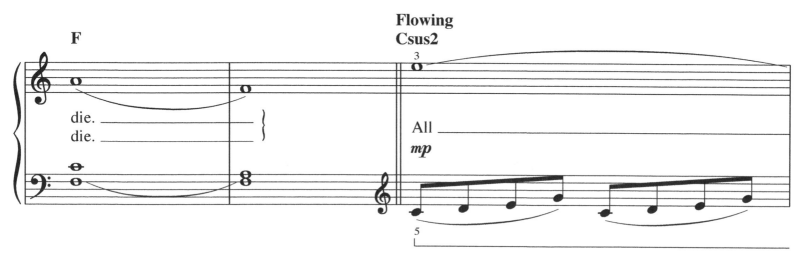

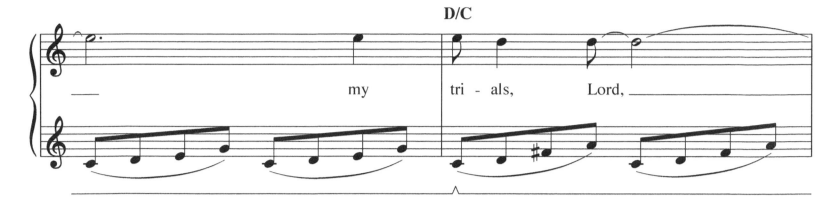

my tri - als, Lord, _____

will soon _____ be

o - ver. _ Too late my broth-ers, _____

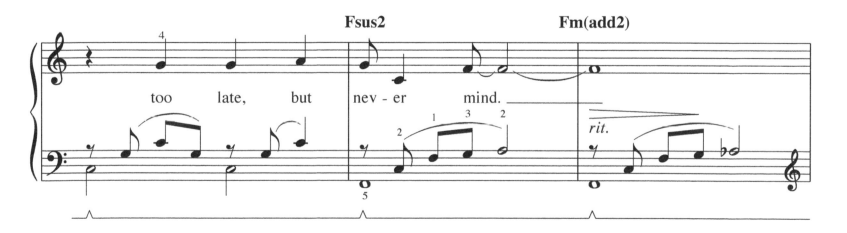

too late, but nev - er mind. _____

Csus2   **D/C**

All _____ my tri - als, Lord, _____

p *a tempo*

5

Fm6/C

_____ will soon _____

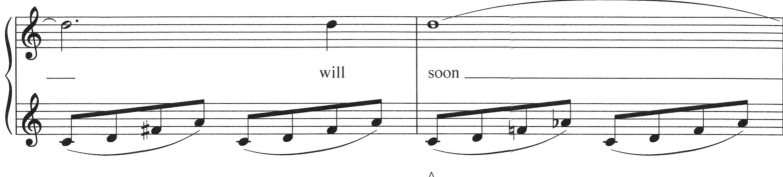

1.
Csus2

_____ be o - ver. _____

rit.

5 4 3 2 1

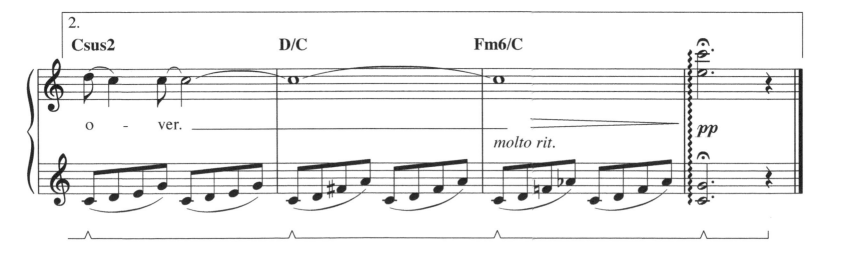

2.
Csus2   **D/C**   **Fm6/C**

o - ver. _____

molto rit.   *pp*

GO DOWN, MOSES

Traditional American Spiritual
Arranged by Phillip Keveren

Slowly, with drama

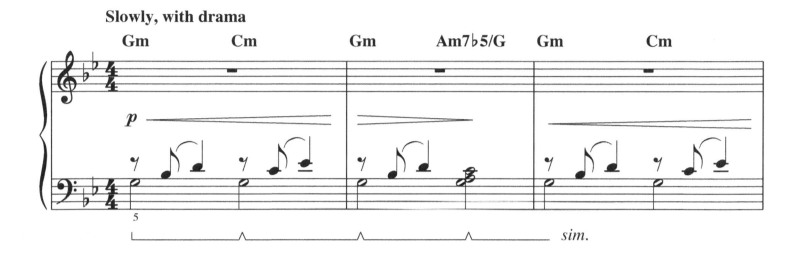

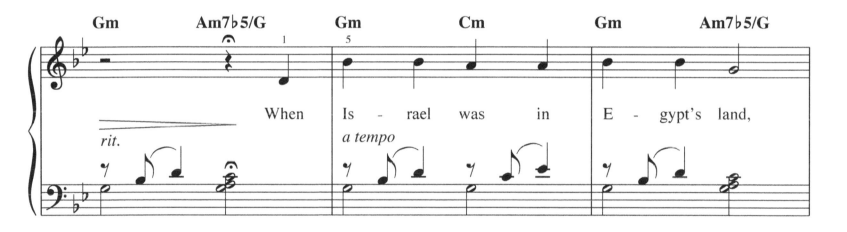

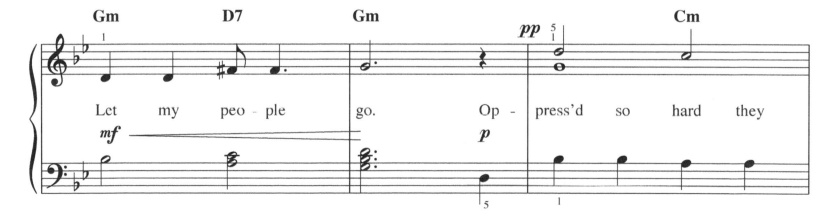

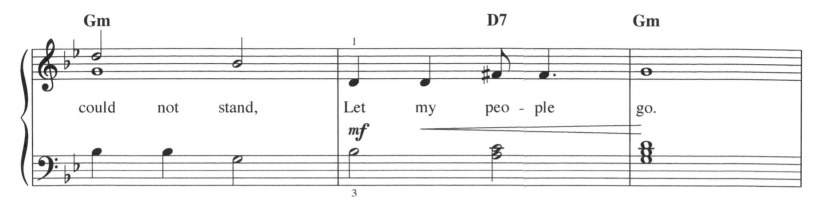

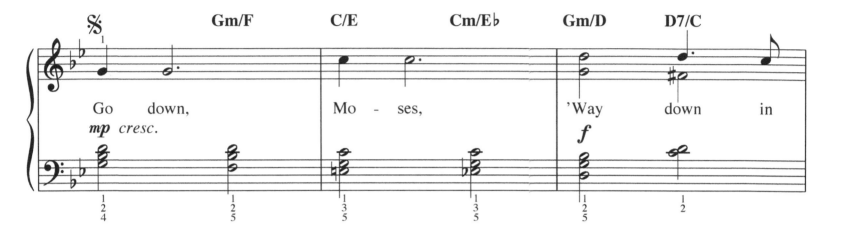

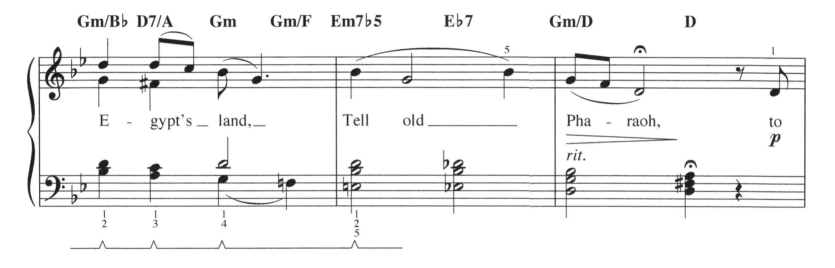

To Coda ⊕

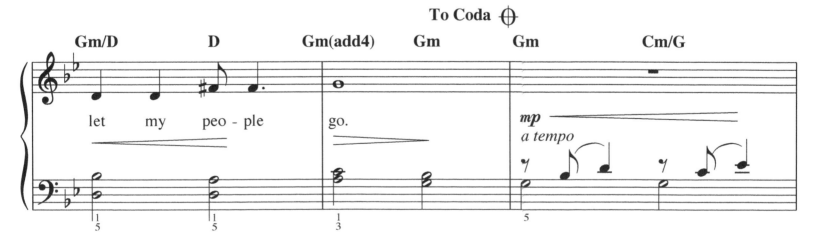

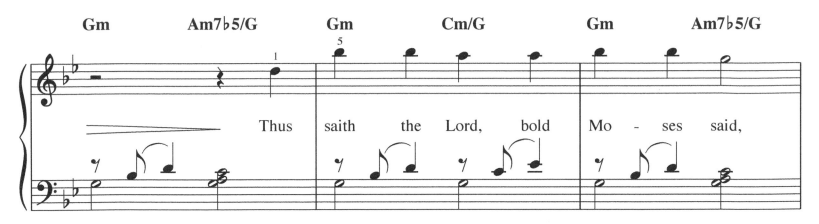

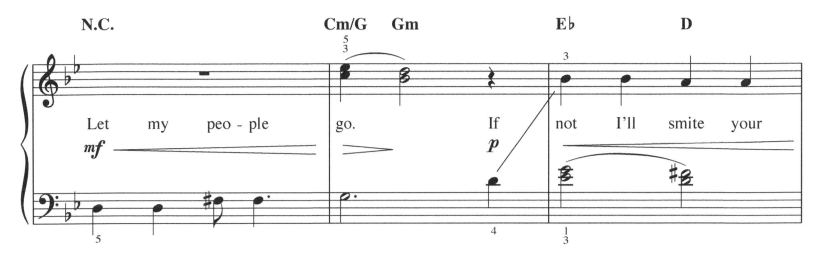

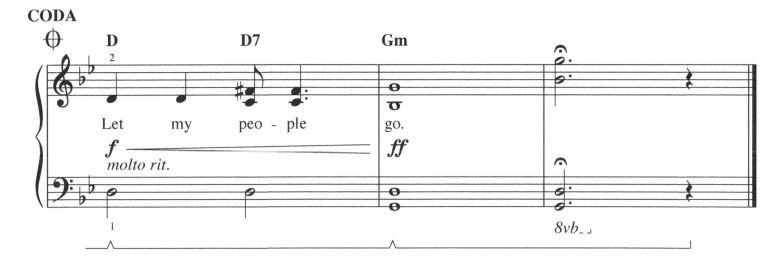

DEEP RIVER

African-American Spiritual
Arranged by Phillip Keveren

Gently flowing

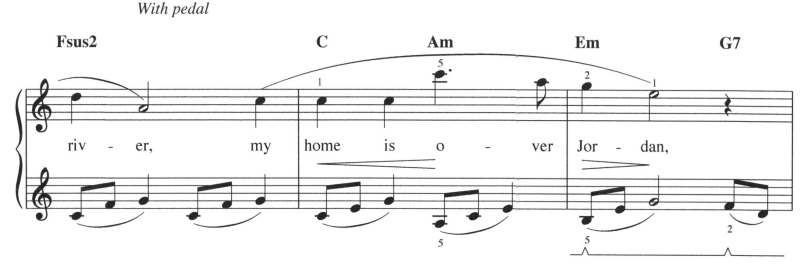

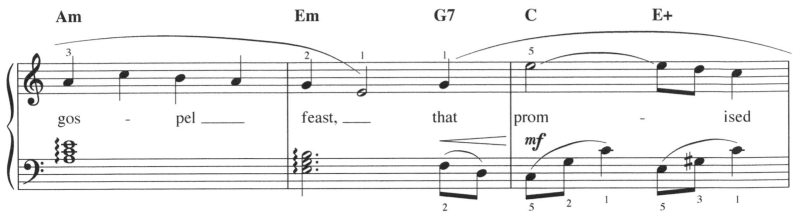

D.S. al Coda

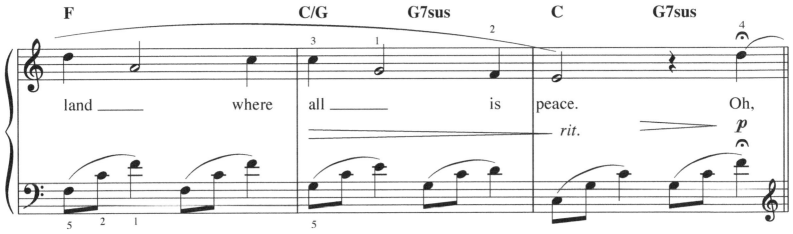

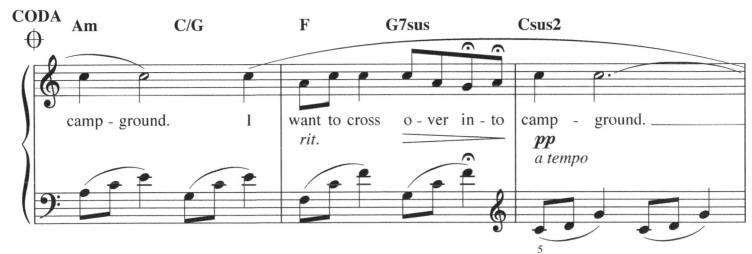

EV'RY TIME I FEEL THE SPIRIT

African-American Spiritual
Arranged by Phillip Keveren

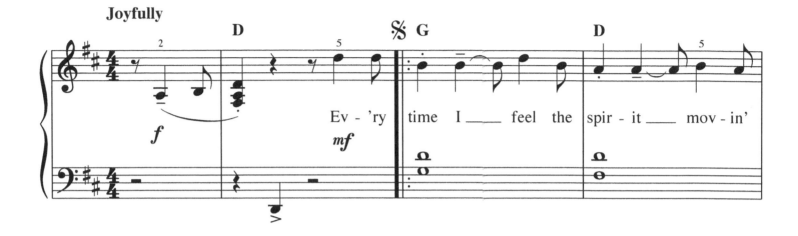

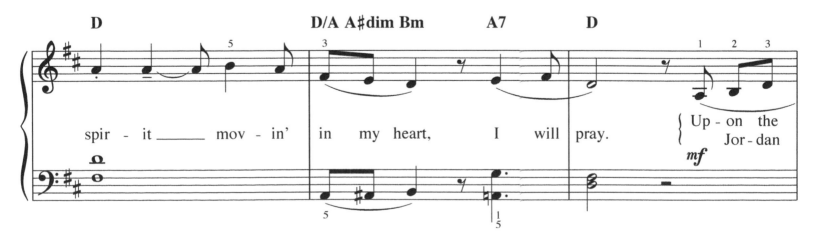

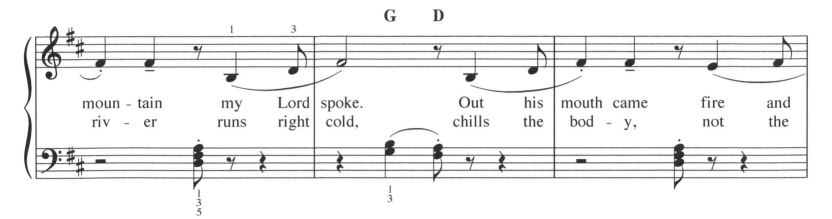

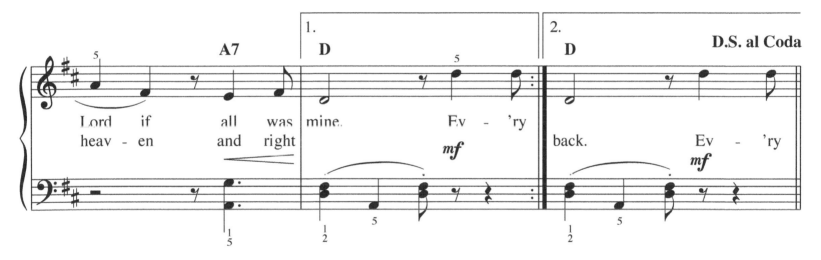

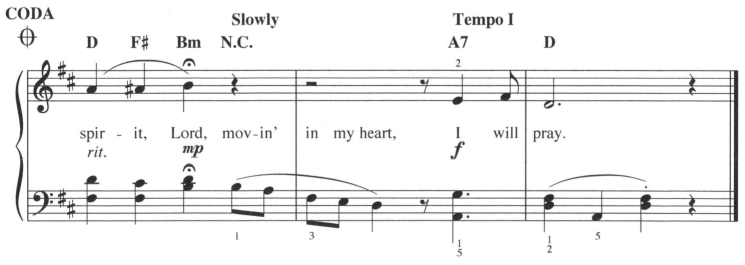

HE'S GOT THE WHOLE WORLD IN HIS HANDS

Traditional Spiritual
Arranged by Phillip Keveren

Relaxed Swing

He's got the whole world _ in His hands; He's got the

whole wide world _ in His hands; He's got the whole world _

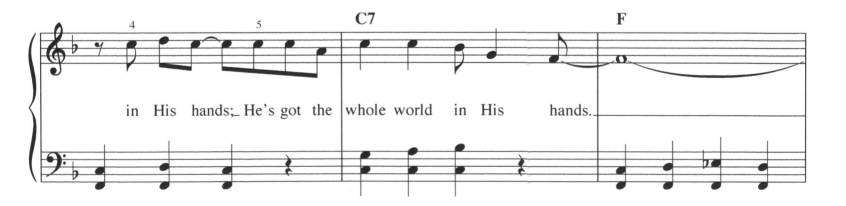

in His hands; He's got the whole world in His hands.

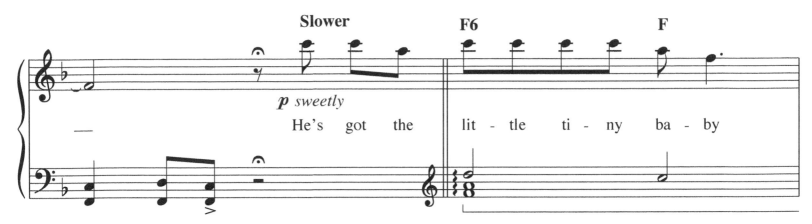

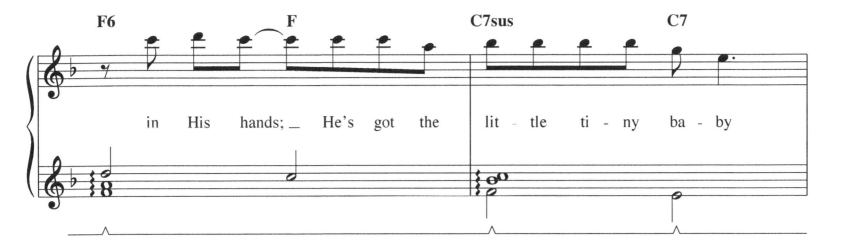

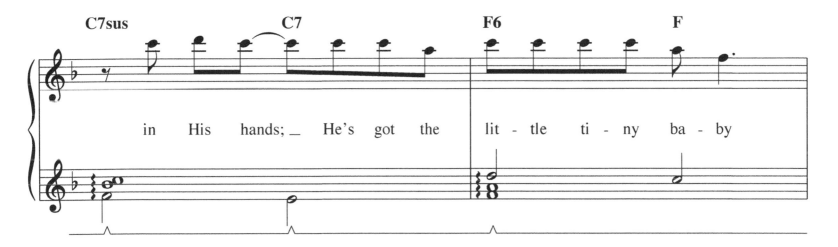

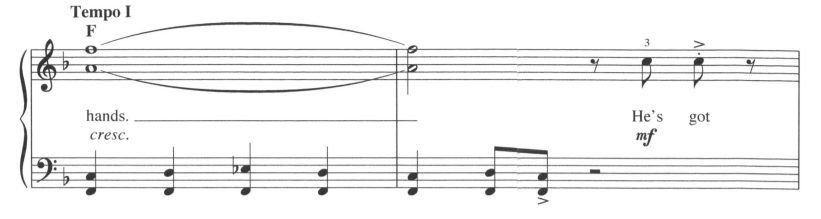

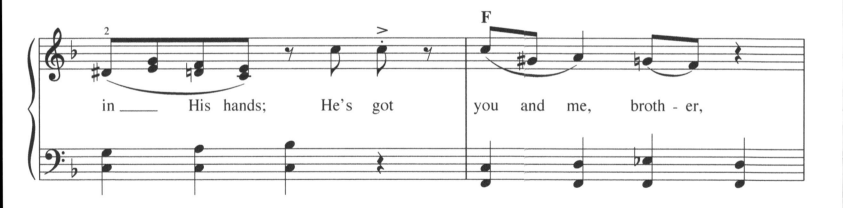

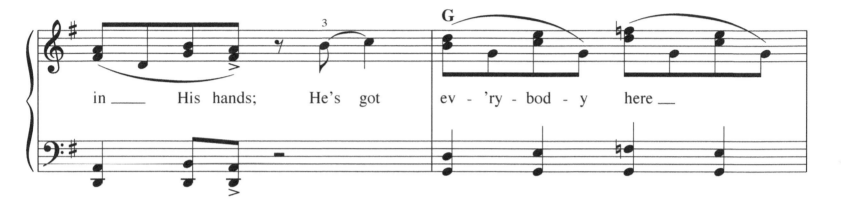

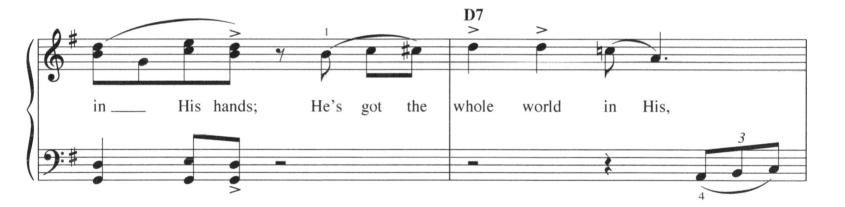

JOSHUA
(Fit the Battle of Jericho)

African-American Spiritual
Arranged by Phillip Keveren

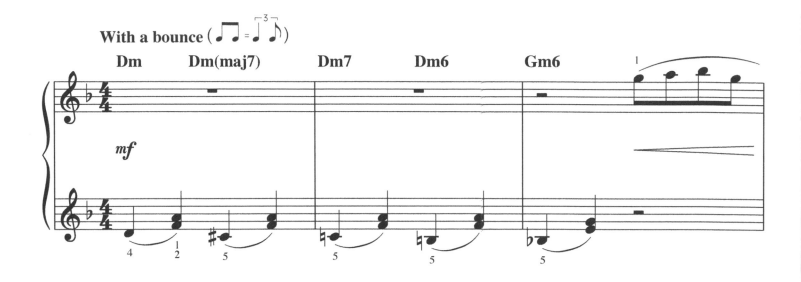

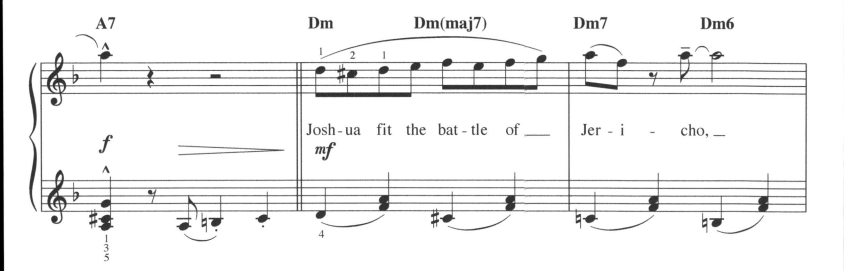

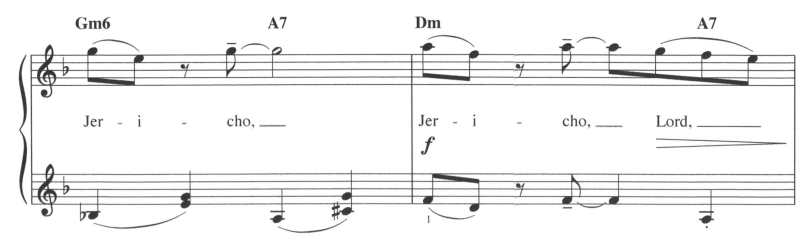

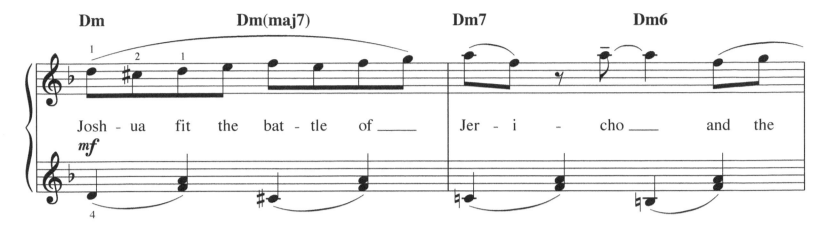

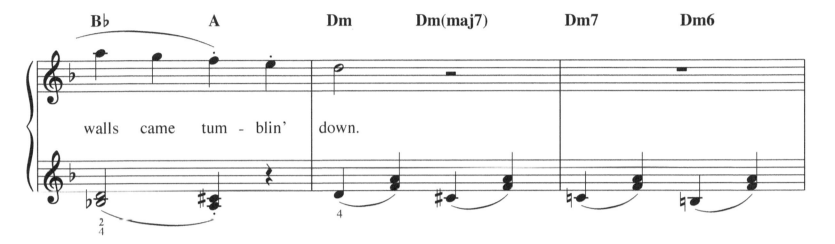

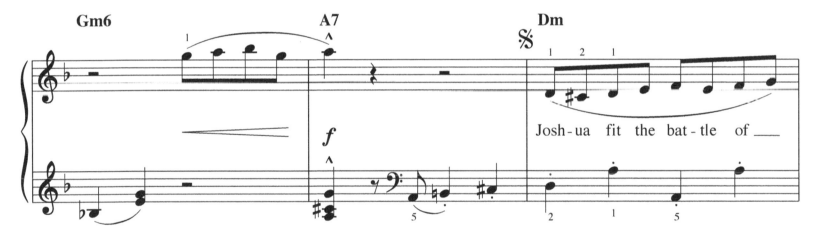

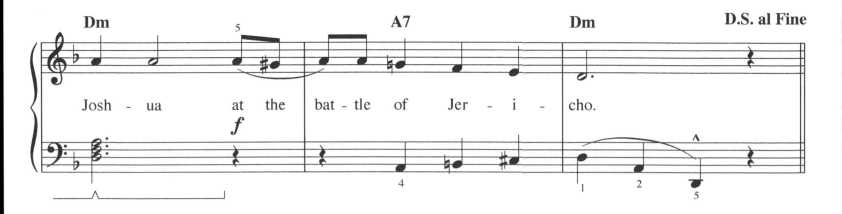

LET US BREAK BREAD TOGETHER

Traditional Spiritual
Arranged by Phillip Keveren

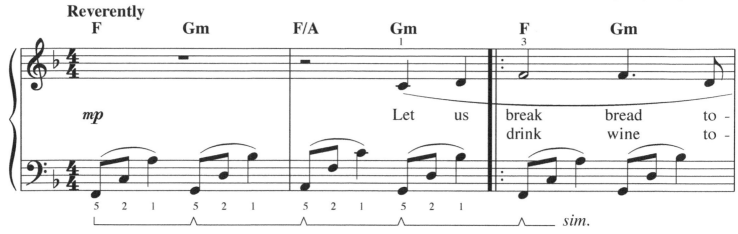

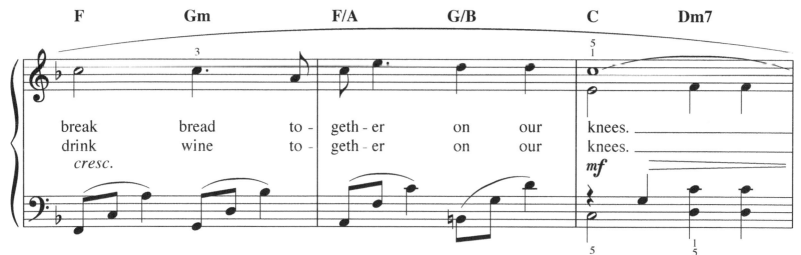

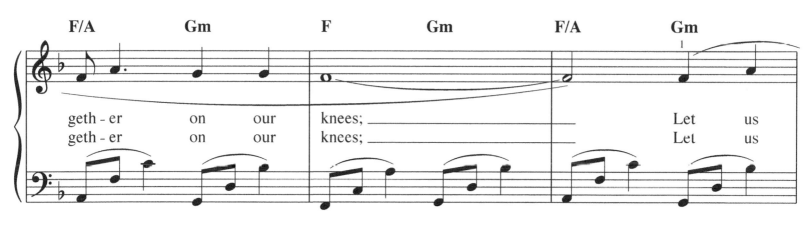

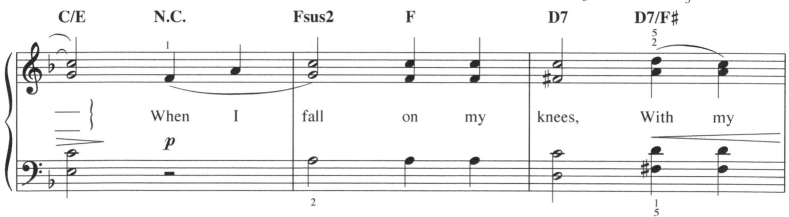

22

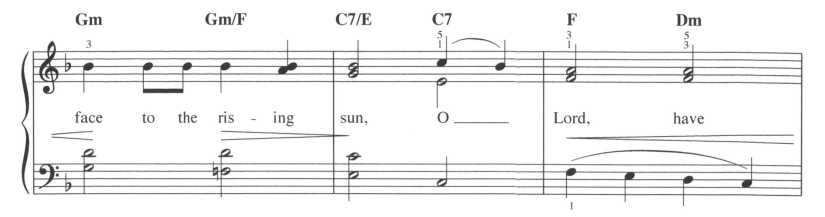

face to the ris - ing sun, O _____ Lord, have

mer - cy on me. _____ Let us

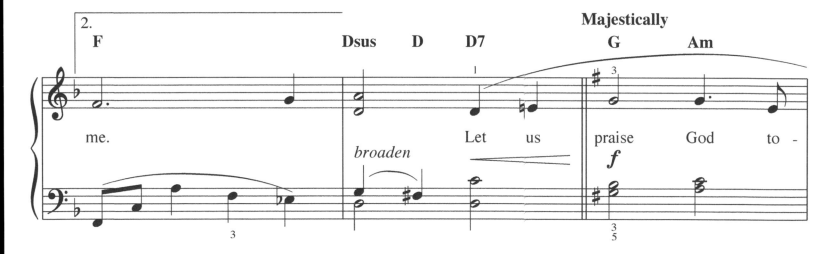

me. _____ Let us praise God to -

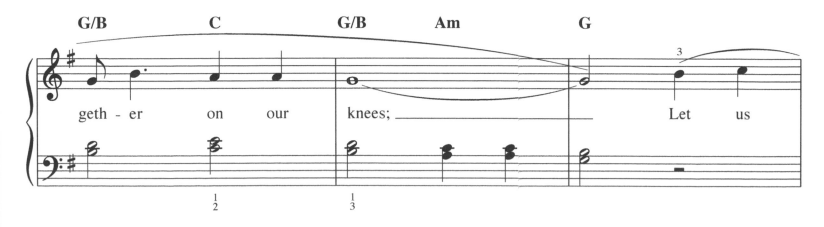

geth - er on our knees; _____ Let us

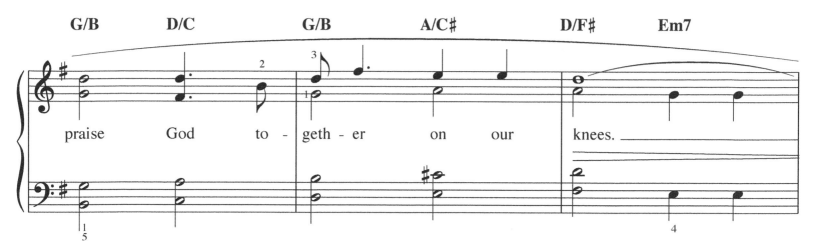

praise God to - geth - er on our knees. _____

_____ When I fall on my knees, With my
mp

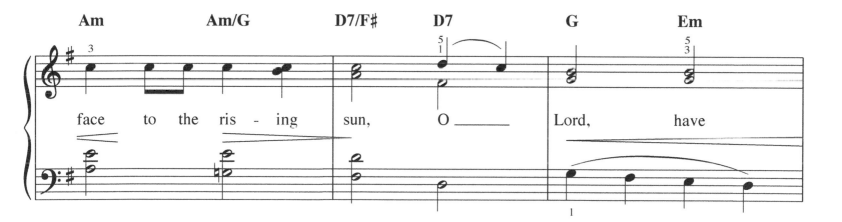

face to the ris - ing sun, O _____ Lord, have

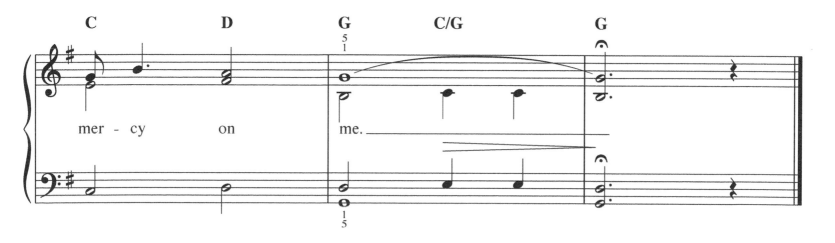

mer - cy on me. _____

THE LONESOME ROAD

African-American Spiritual
Arranged by Phillip Keveren

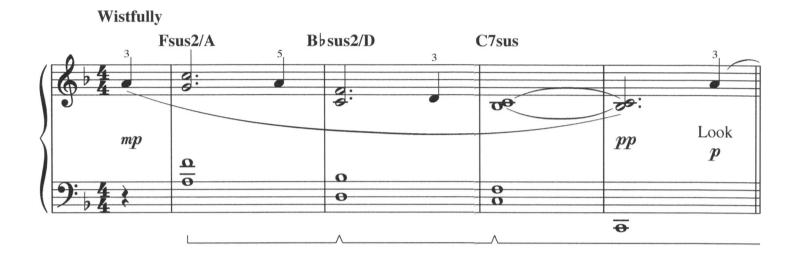

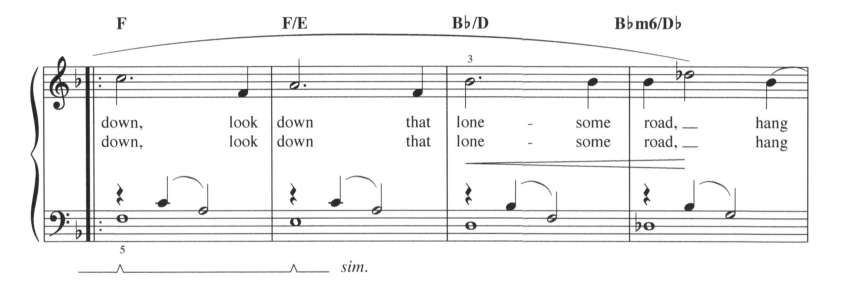

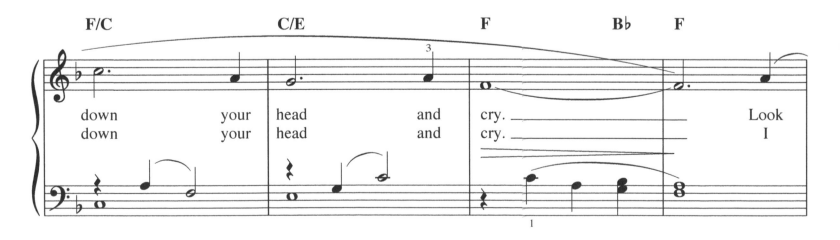

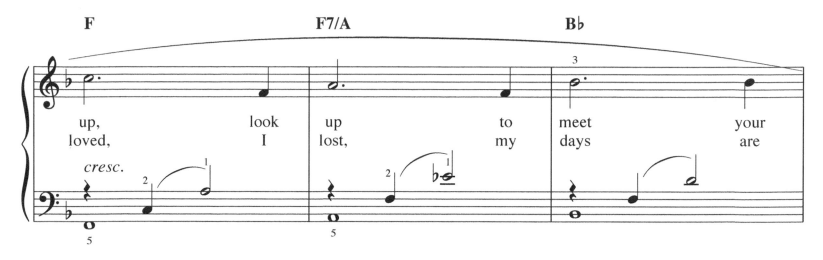

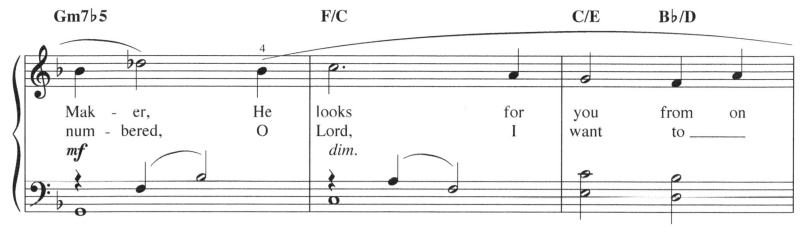

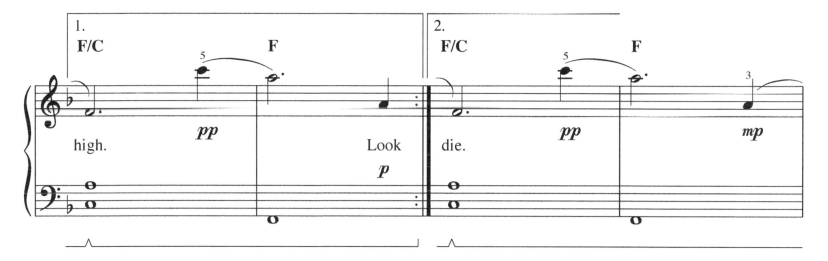

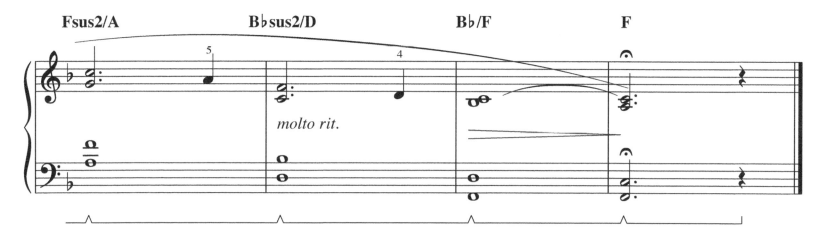

OH FREEDOM

African-American Spiritual
Arranged by Phillip Keveren

Slowly, expressively

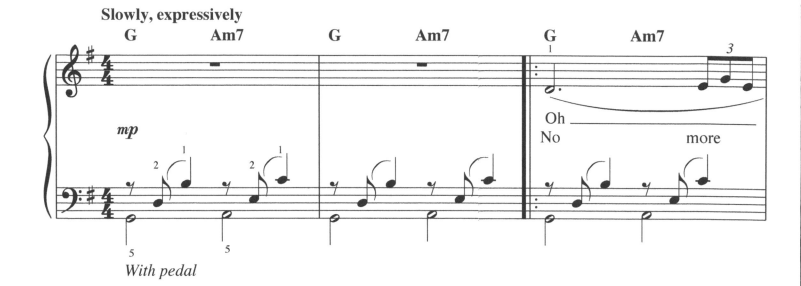

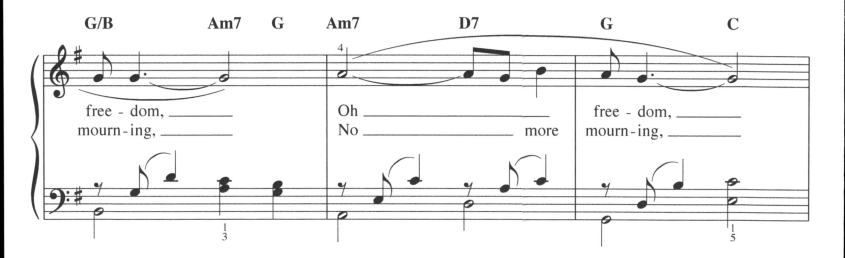

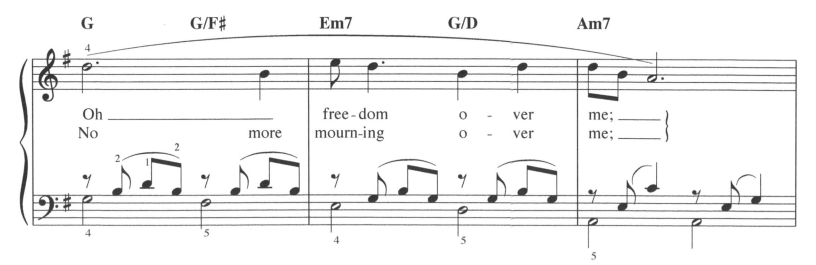

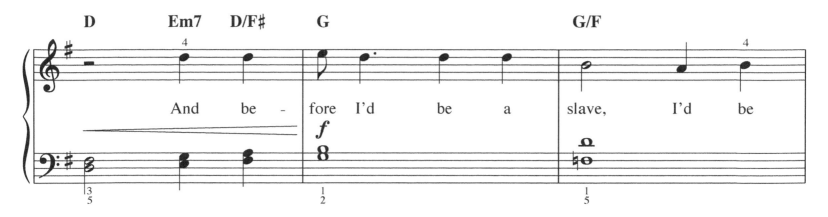

And be - fore I'd be a slave, I'd be

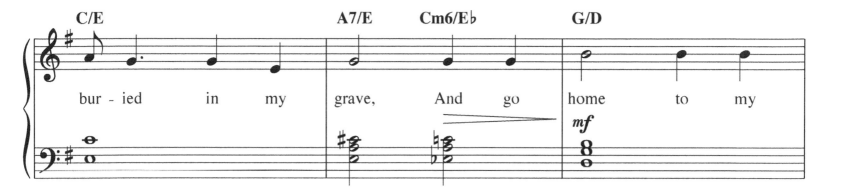

bur - ied in my grave, And go home to my

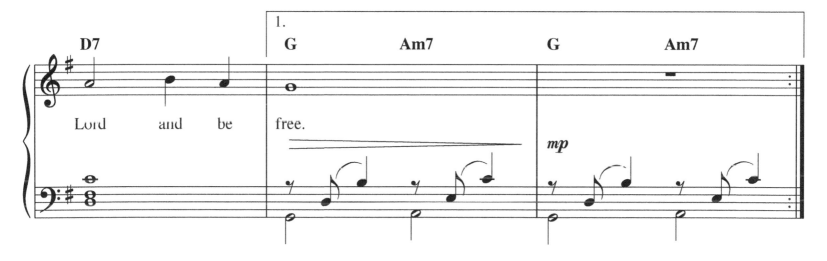

Lord and be free.

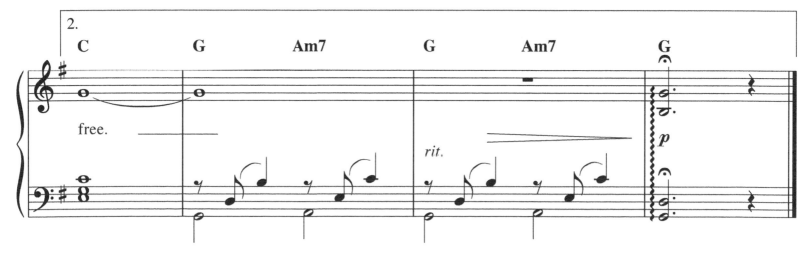

free.

ROCK-A-MY SOUL

African-American Spiritual
Arranged by Phillip Keveren

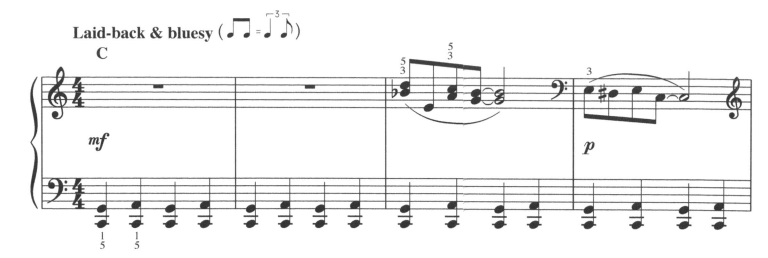

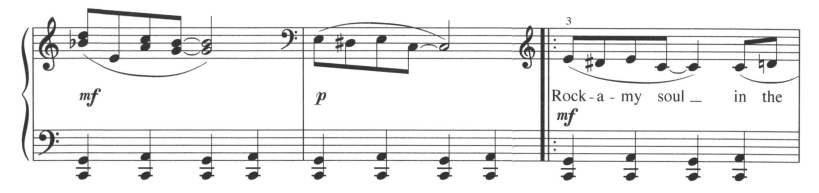

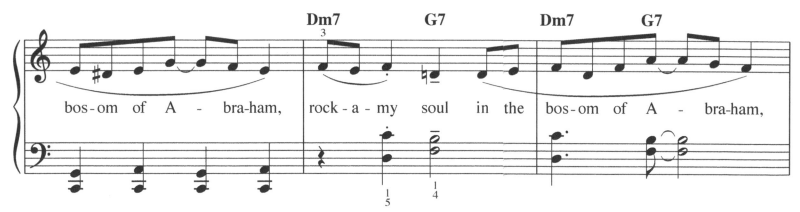

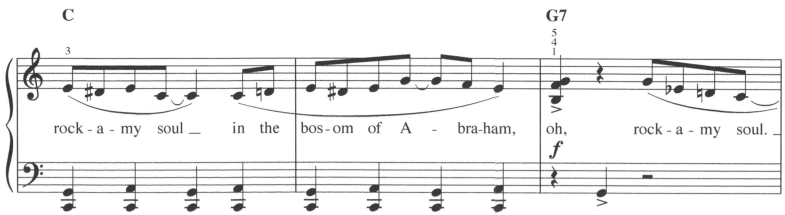

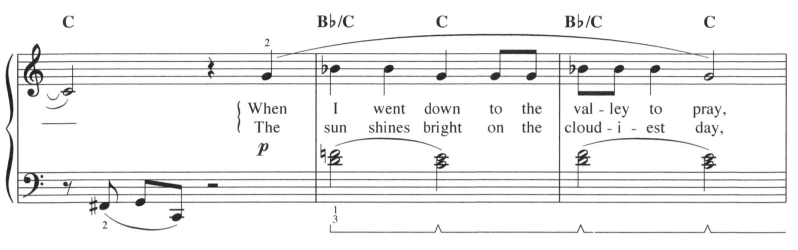

When I went down to the val - ley to pray,
The sun shines bright on the cloud - i - est day,

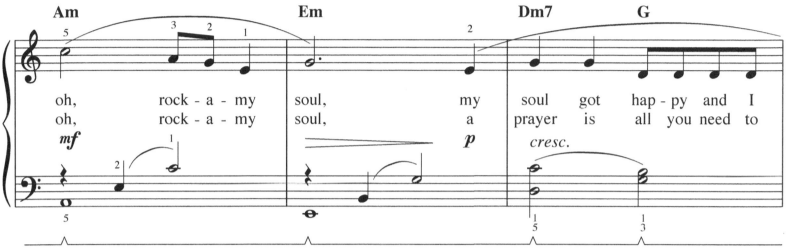

oh, rock - a - my soul, my soul got hap - py and I
oh, rock - a - my soul, a prayer is all you need to

stayed all day,
light your way,

oh, rock - a - my soul.

2.

oh, rock - a - my soul!

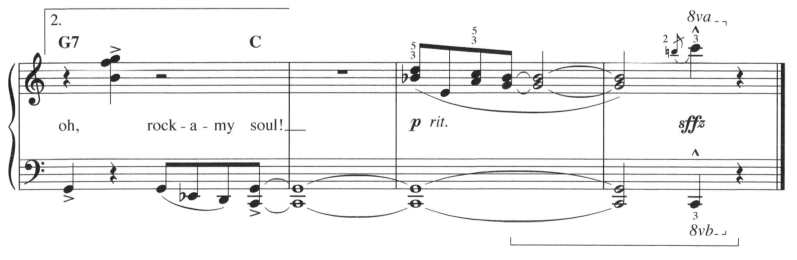

SOMEBODY'S KNOCKIN' AT YOUR DOOR

African-American Spiritual
Arranged by Phillip Keveren

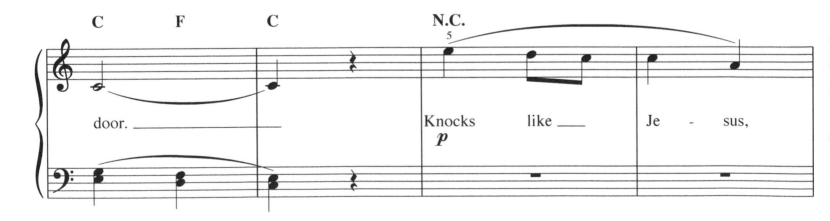

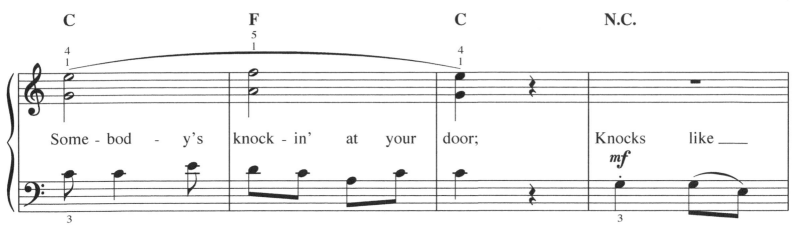

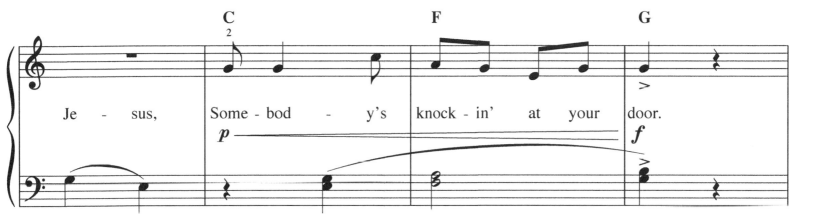

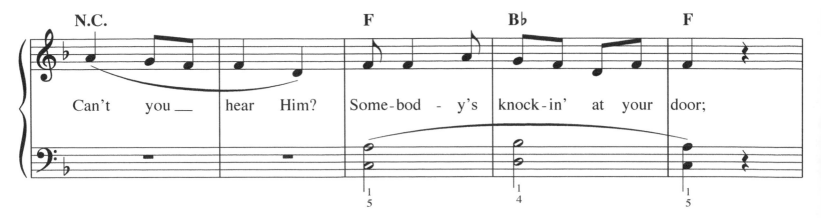

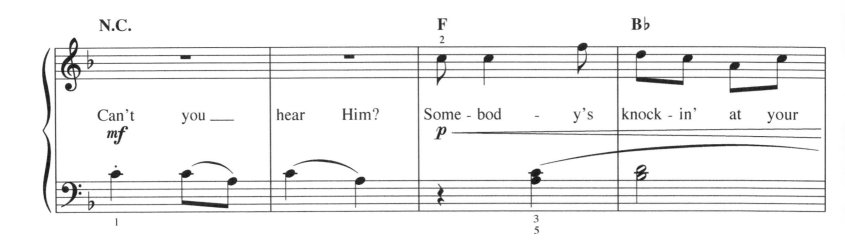

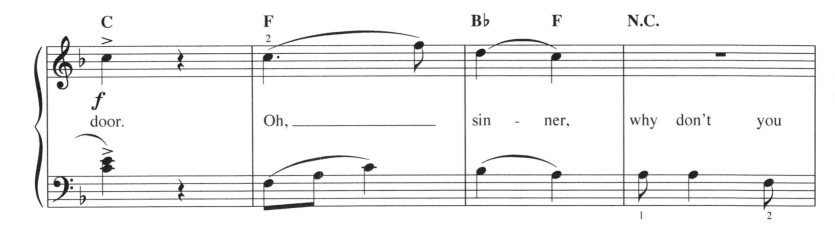

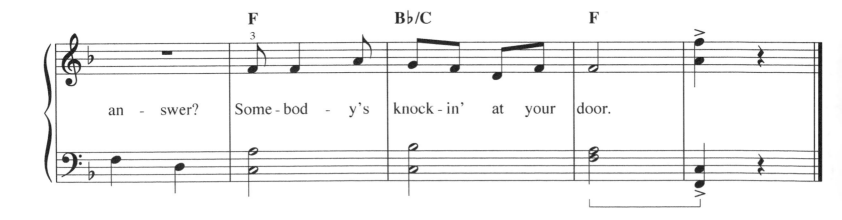

SOMETIMES I FEEL LIKE A MOTHERLESS CHILD

Traditional
Arranged by Phillip Keveren

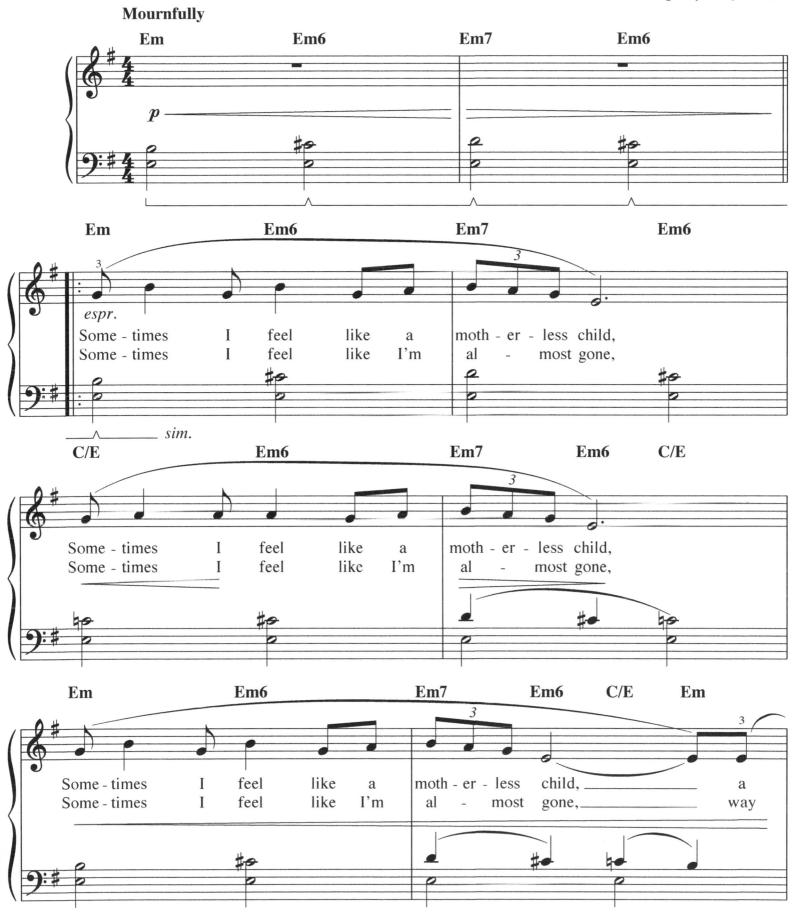

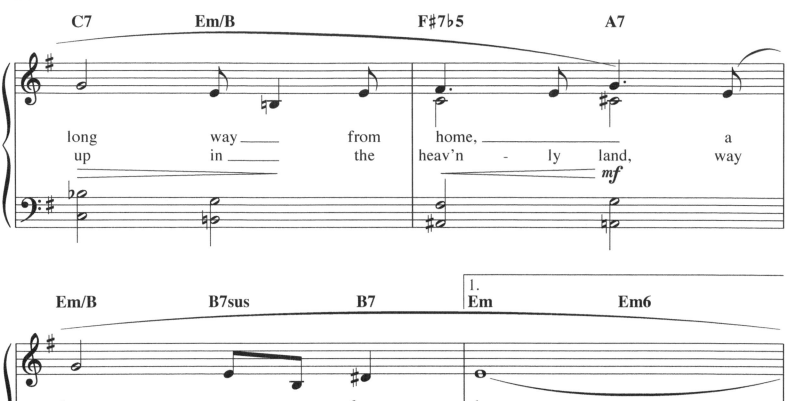

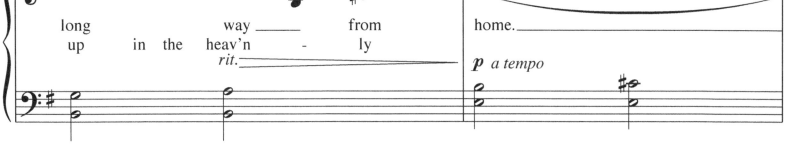

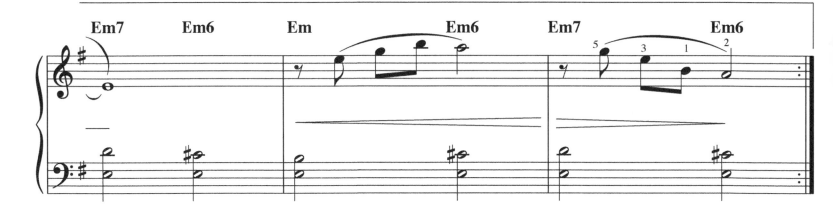

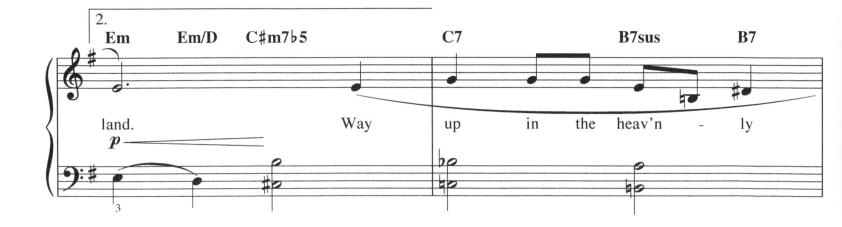

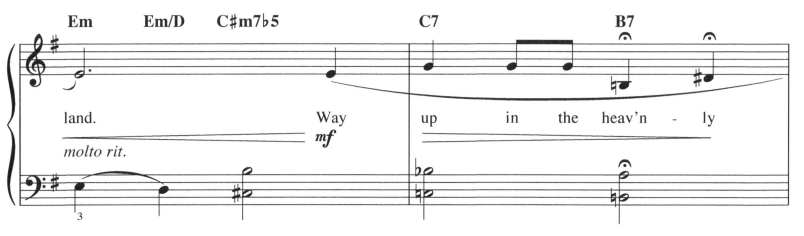

land.

Way up in the heav'n - ly

molto rit. *mf*

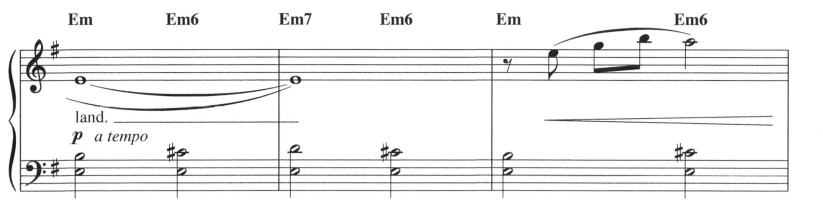

land.

p a tempo

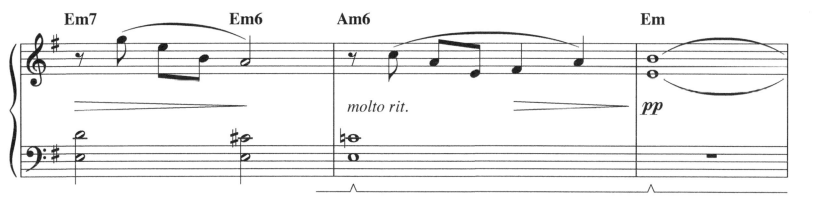

molto rit. *pp*

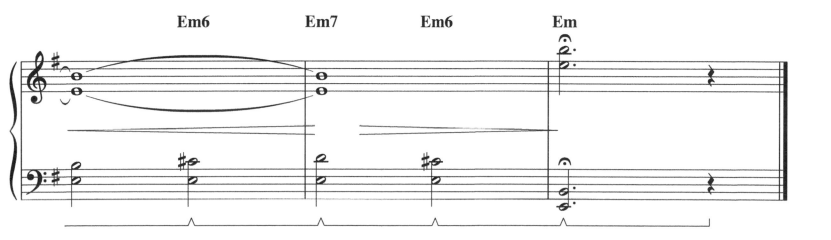

SOON AH WILL BE DONE

African-American Spiritual
Arranged by Phillip Keveren

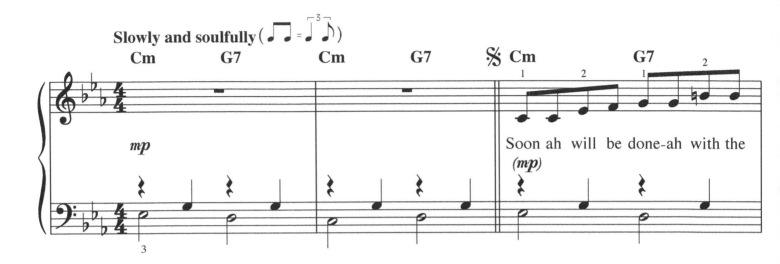

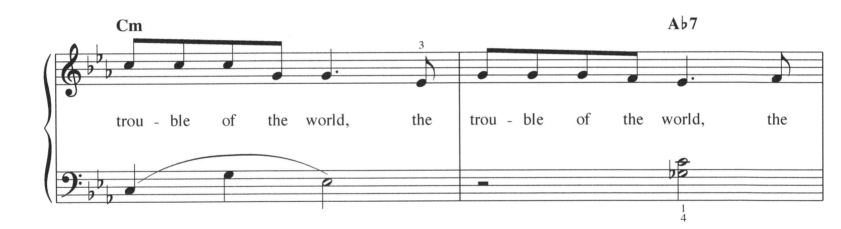

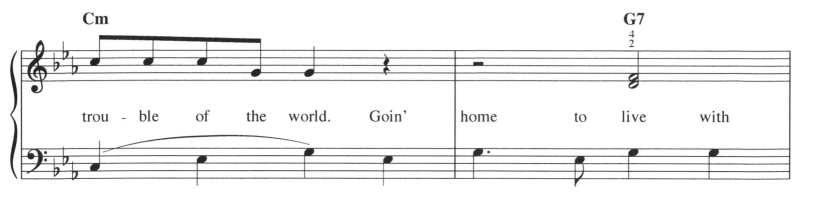

trou - ble of the world. Goin' home to live with

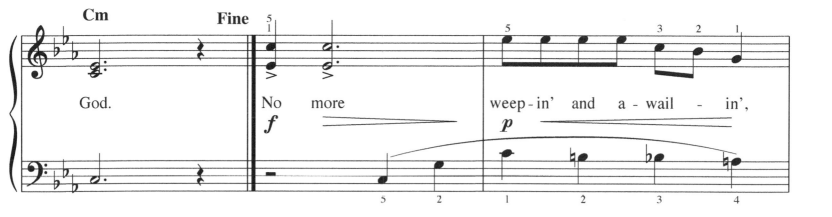

God. No more weep-in' and a-wail - in',

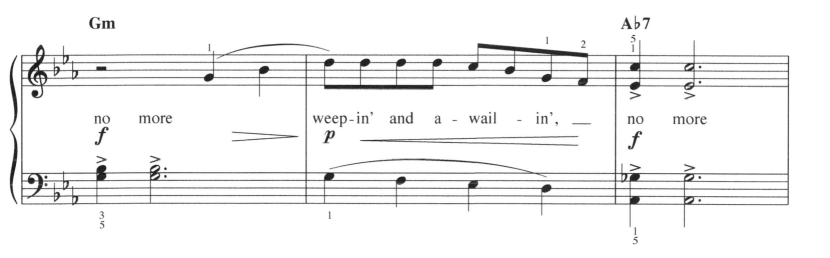

no more weep-in' and a - wail - in', __ no more

weep-in' and a - wail - in', I'm goin' to live with God.

STEAL AWAY
(Steal Away to Jesus)

Traditional Spiritual
Arranged by Phillip Keveren

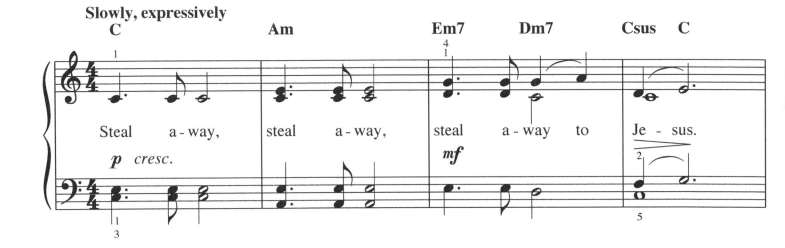

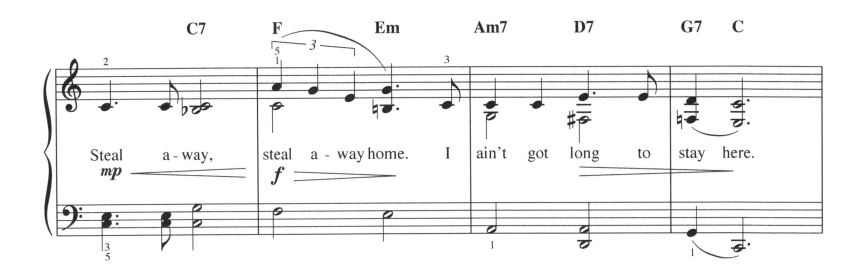

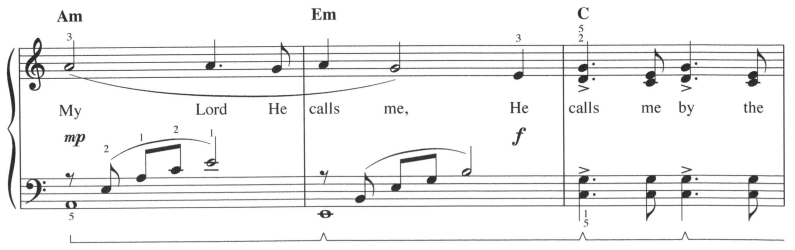

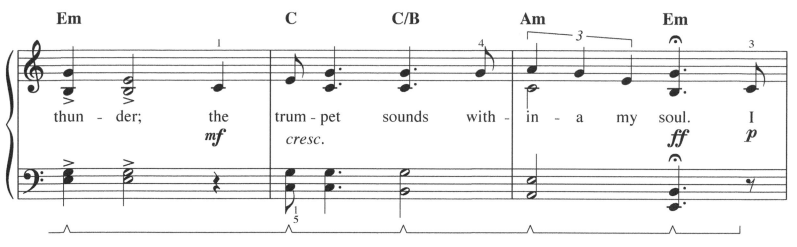

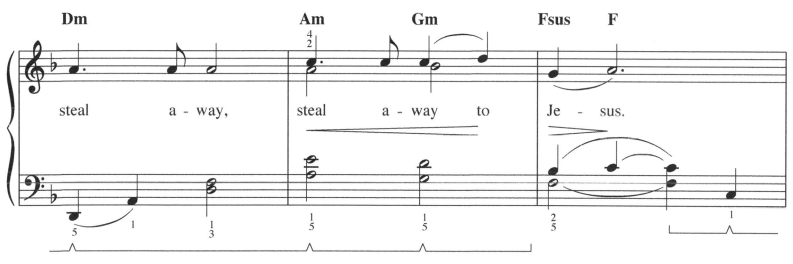

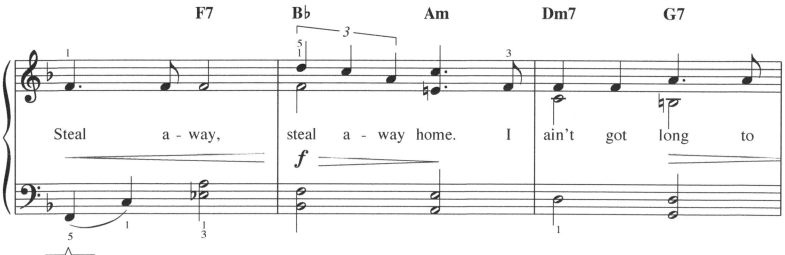

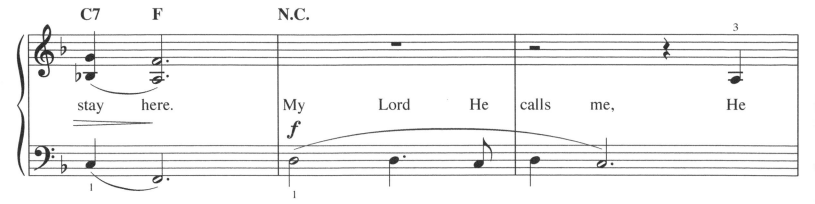

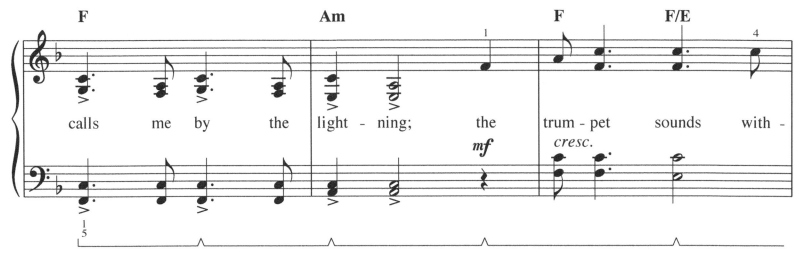

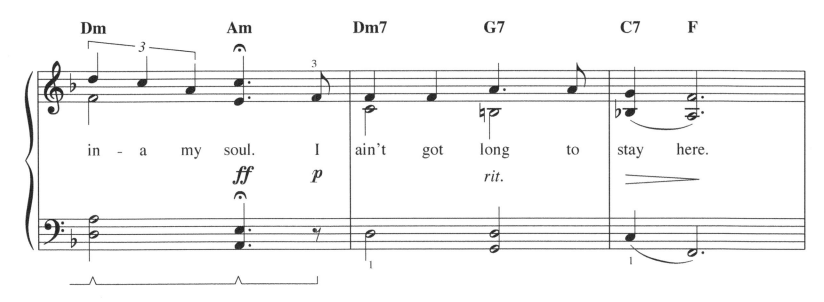

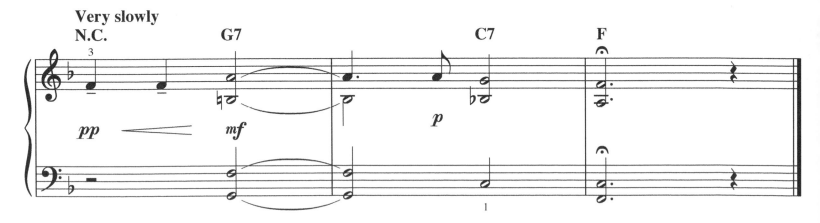

WAYFARING STRANGER

Southern American Folk Hymn
Arranged by Phillip Keveren

Slowly, mournfully

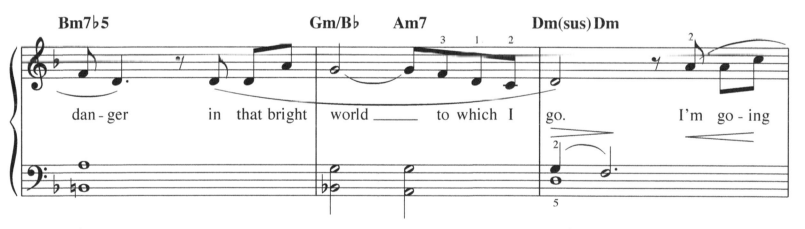

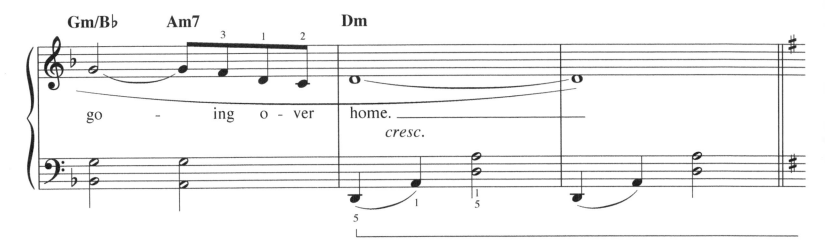

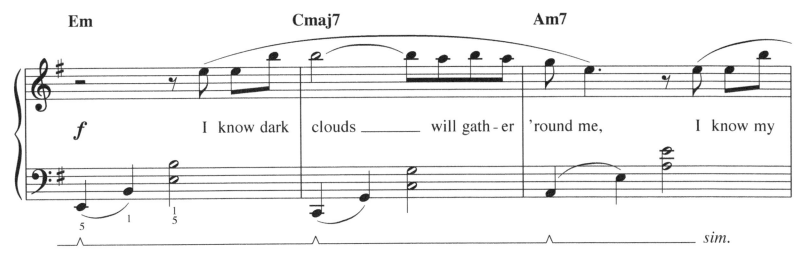

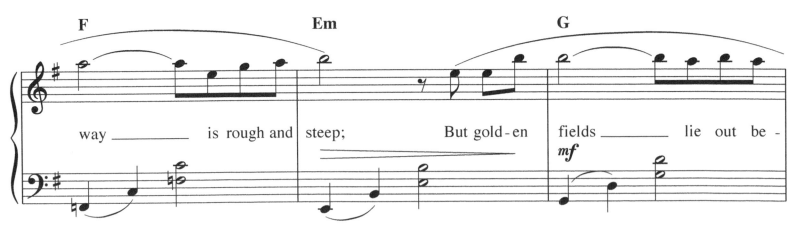

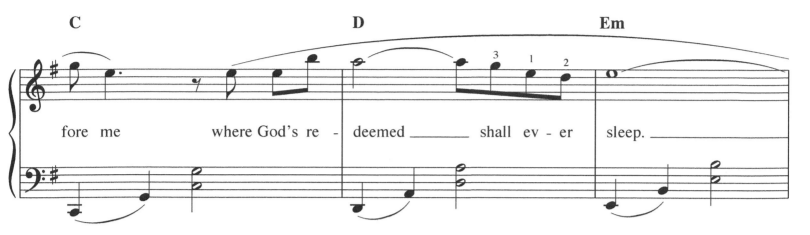

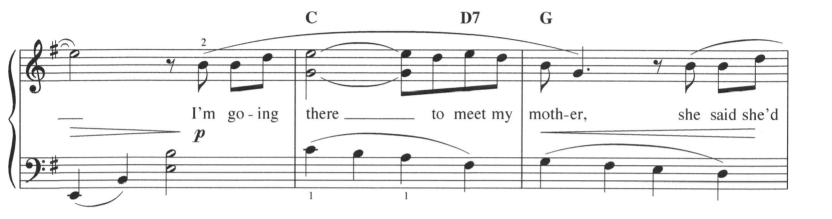

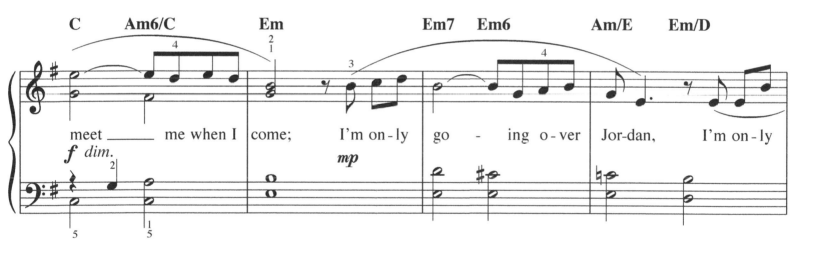

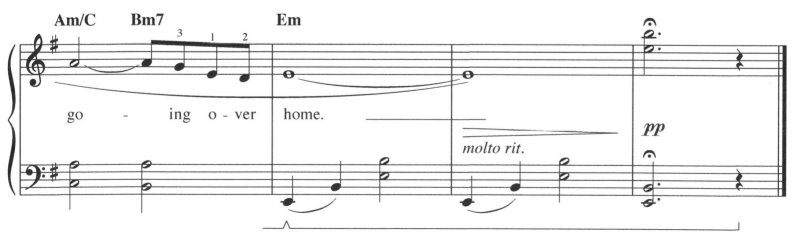

SWING LOW, SWEET CHARIOT

Traditional Spiritual
Arranged by Phillip Keveren

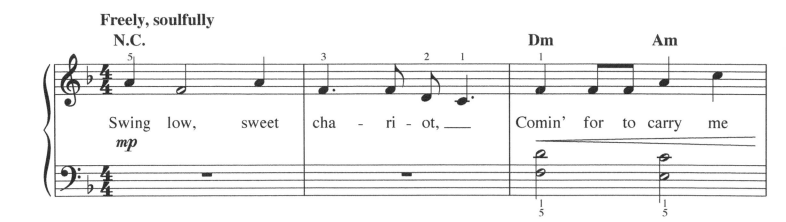

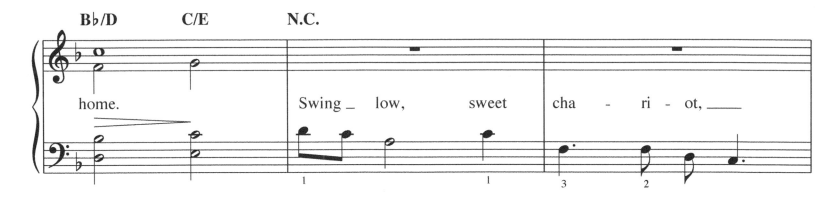

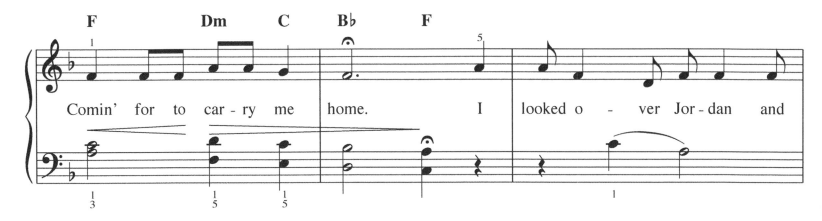

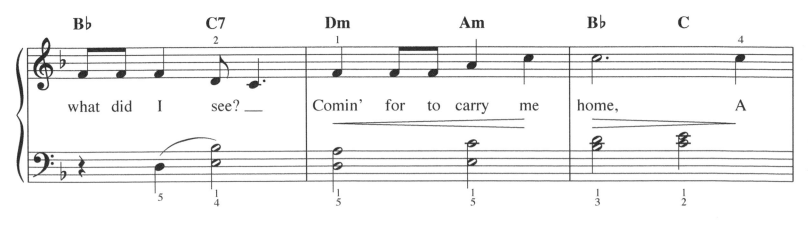

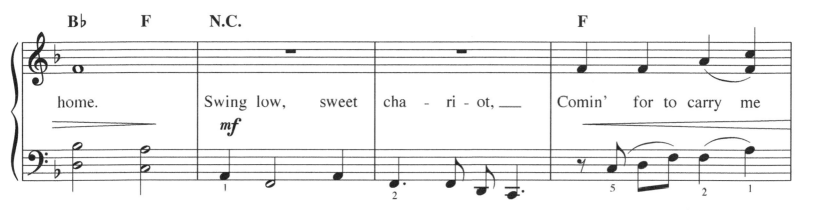

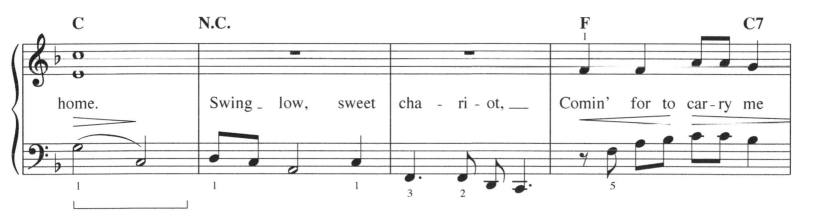

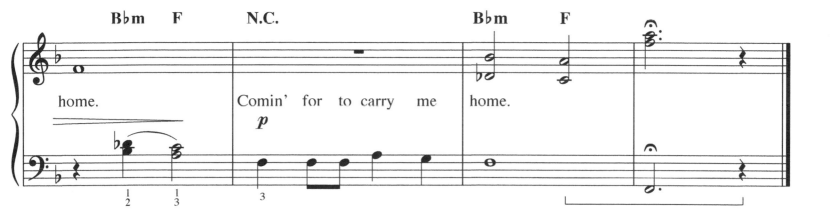

THERE IS A BALM IN GILEAD

African-American Spiritual
Arranged by Phillip Keveren

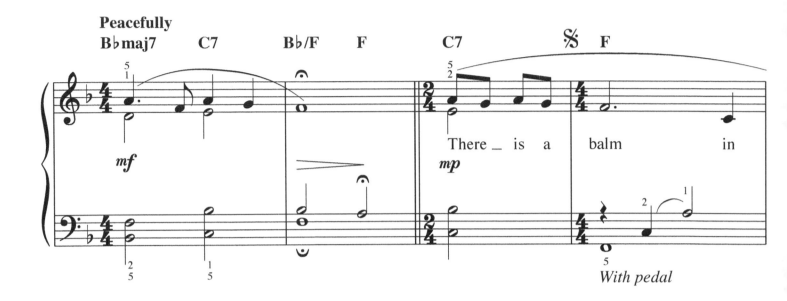

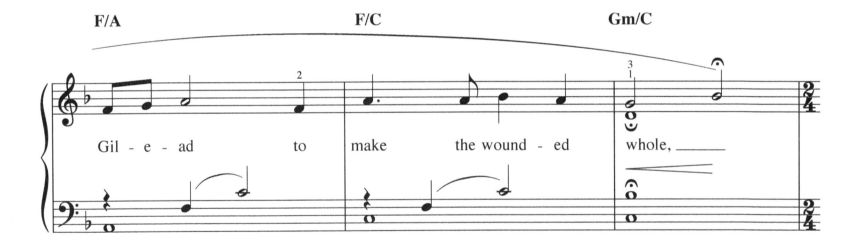

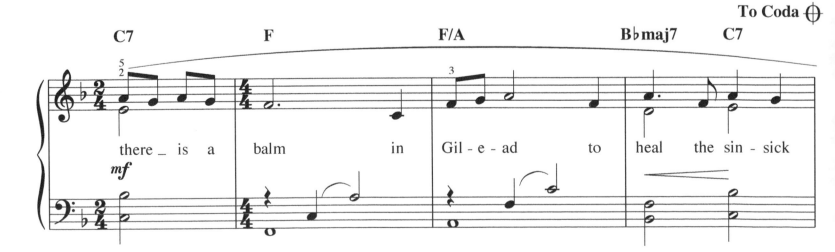

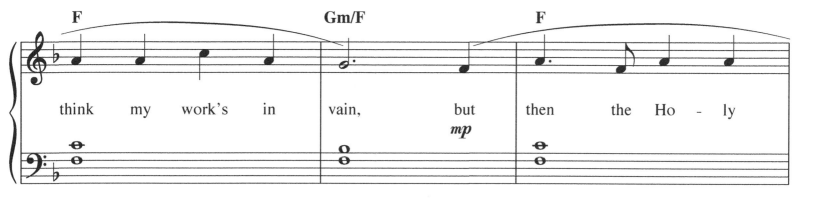

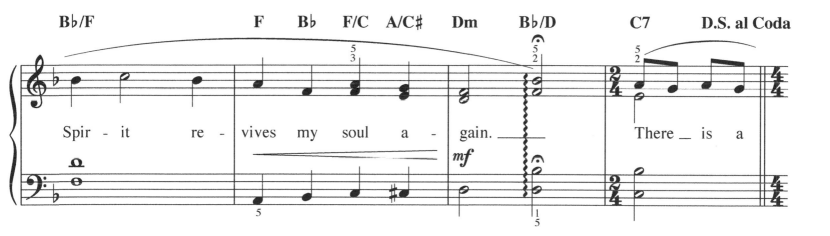

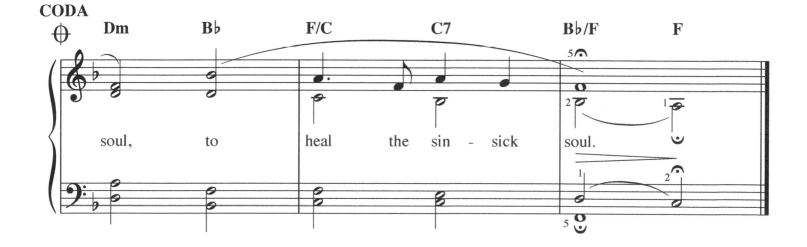

THIS LITTLE LIGHT OF MINE

African-American Spiritual
Arranged by Phillip Keveren

Joyfully

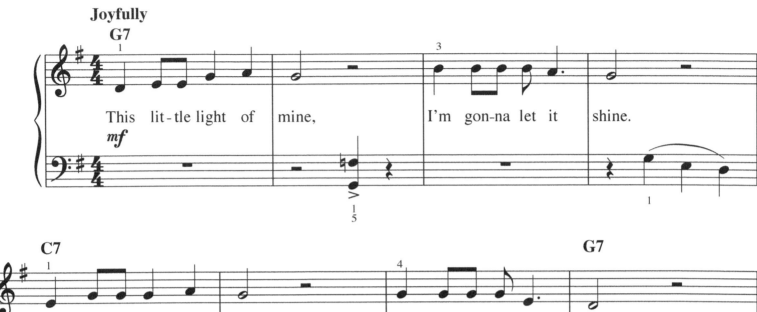

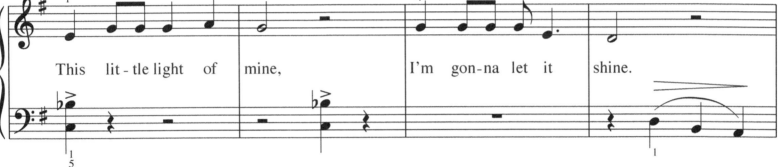

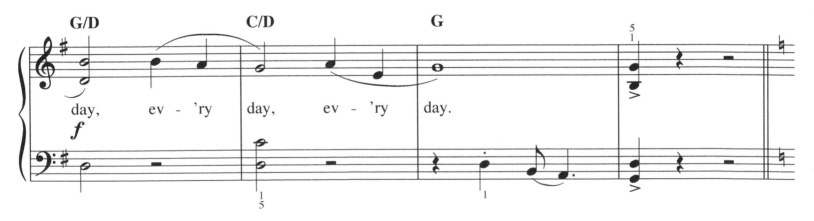

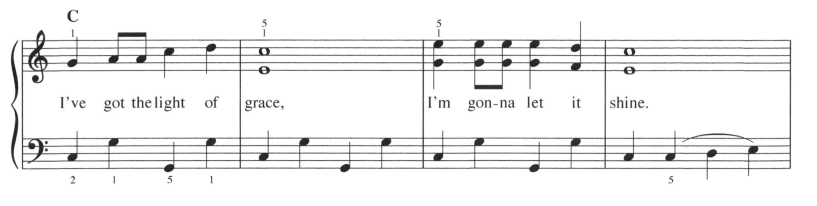

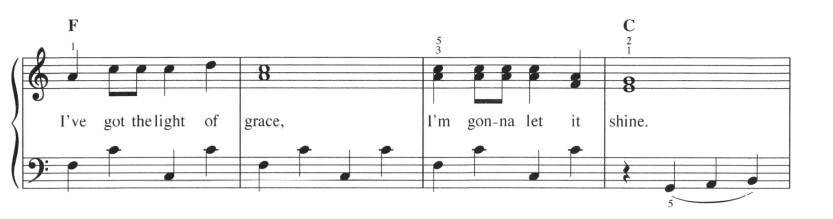

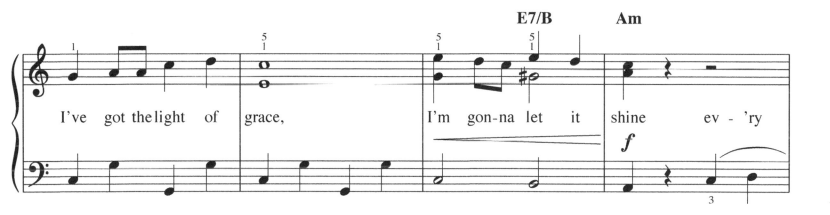

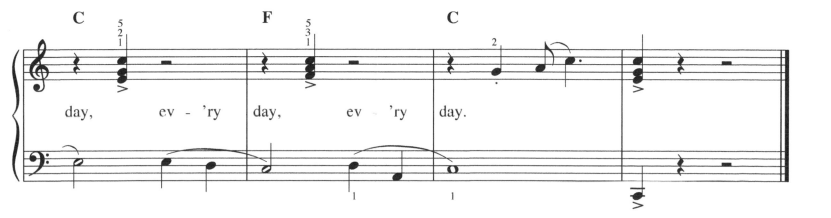

WERE YOU THERE?

Traditional Spiritual
Arranged by Phillip Keveren

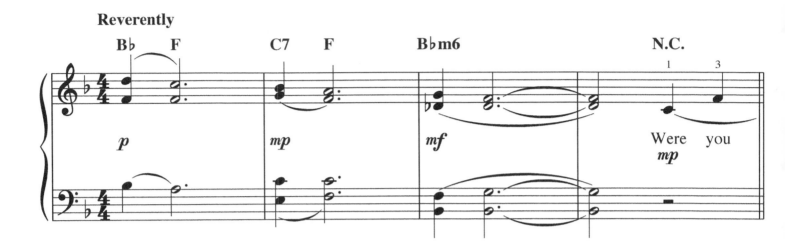

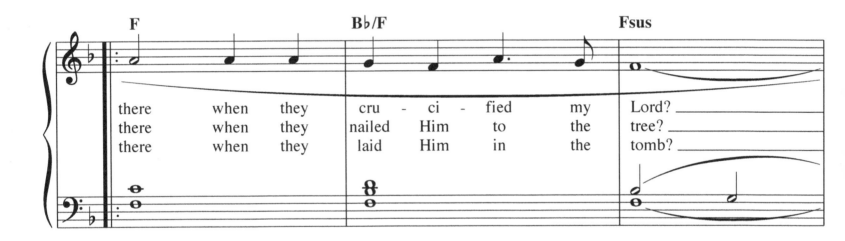

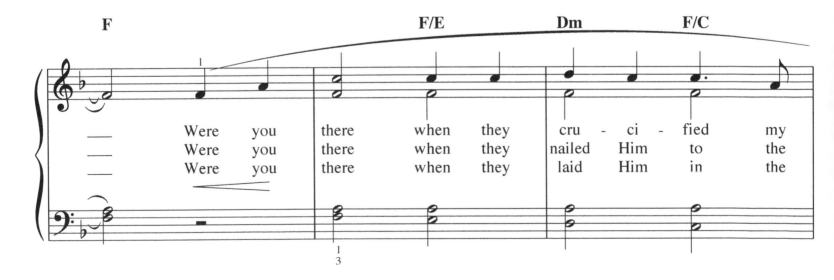

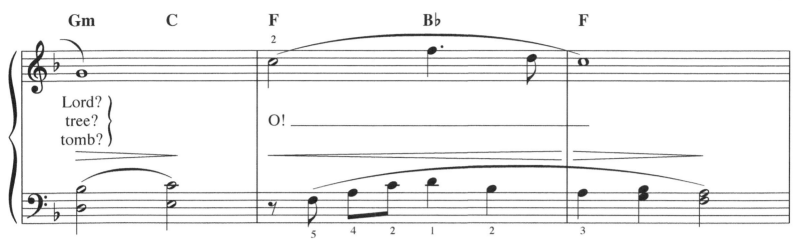

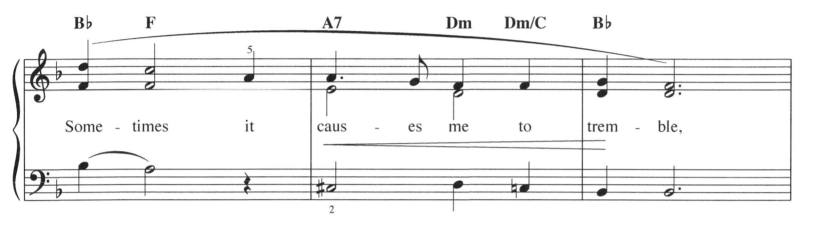

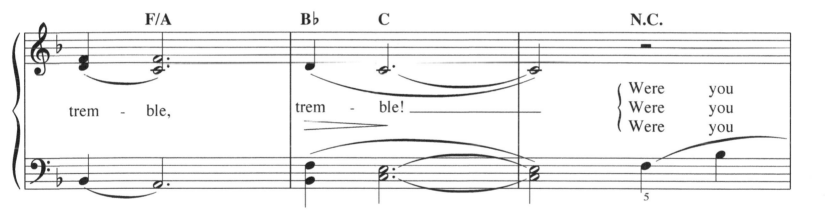

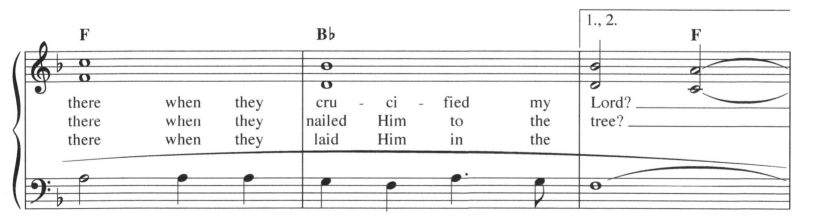

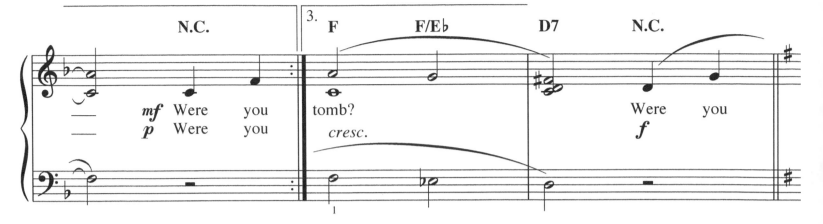

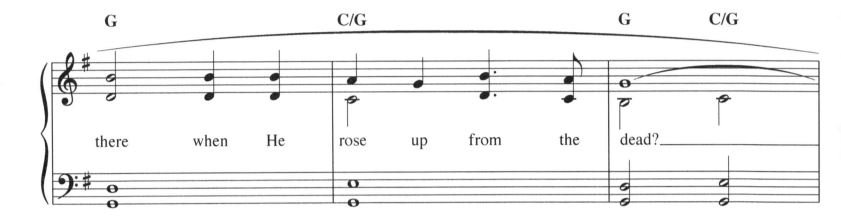

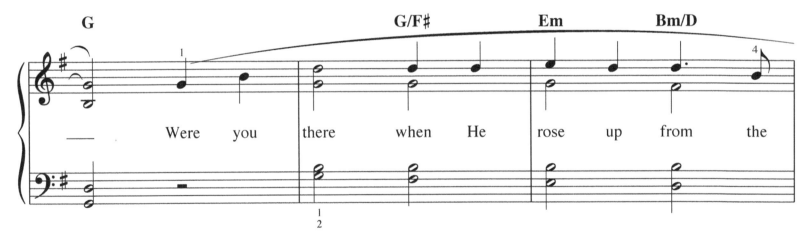

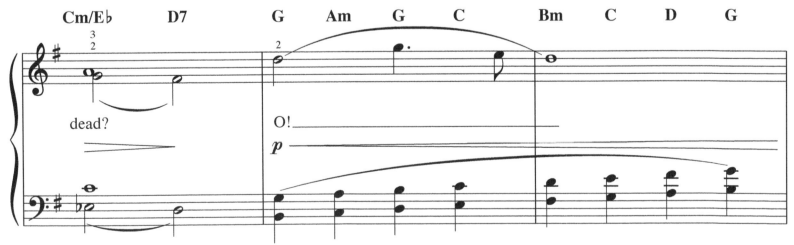

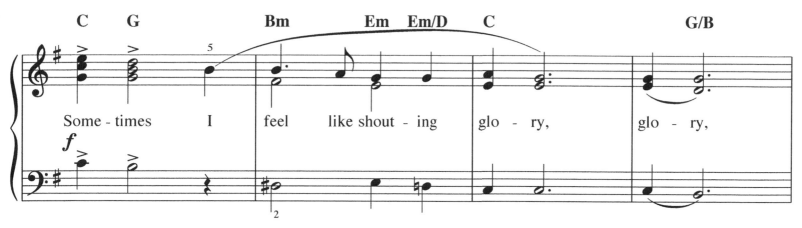

Some - times I feel like shout - ing glo - ry, glo - ry,

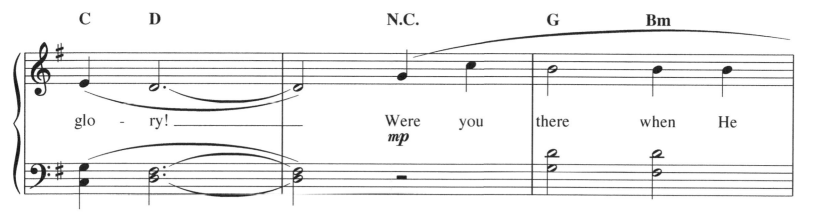

glo - ry! Were you there when He

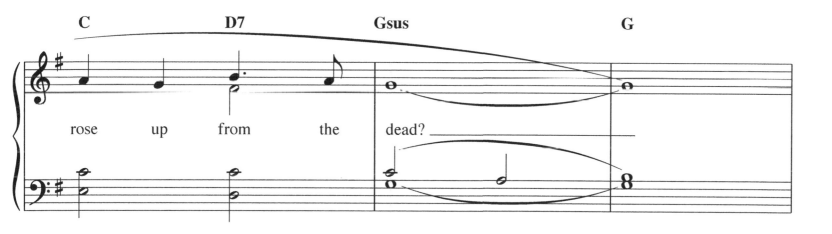

rose up from the dead?

Very slowly

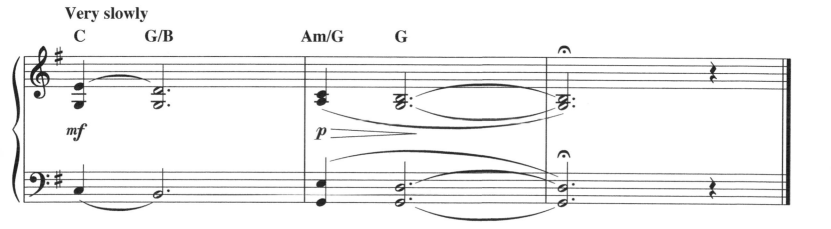

WE ARE CLIMBING JACOB'S LADDER

African-American Spiritual
Arranged by Phillip Keveren

Slowly, steadily

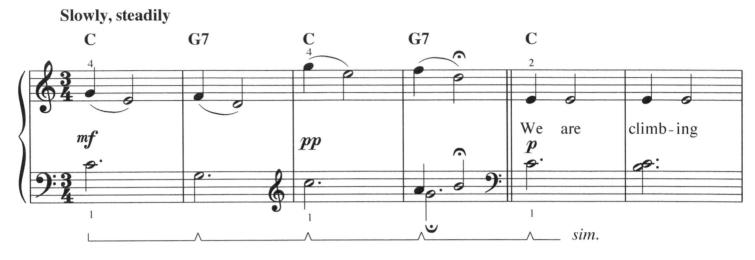

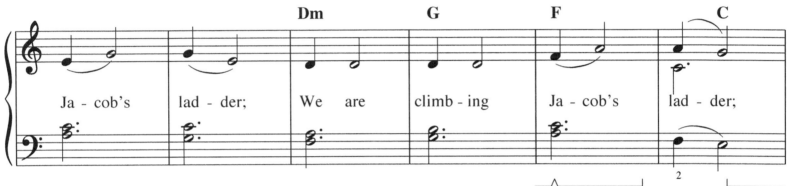

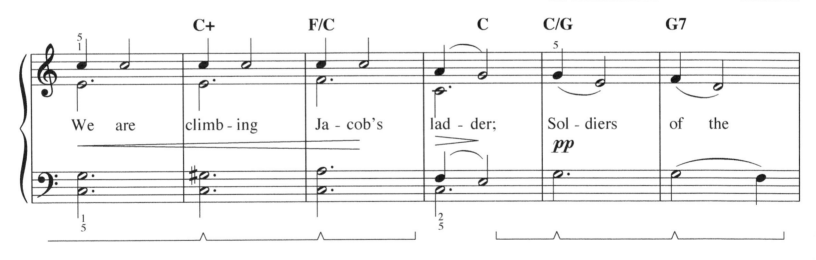

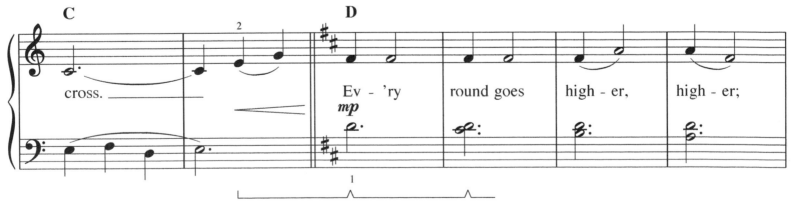

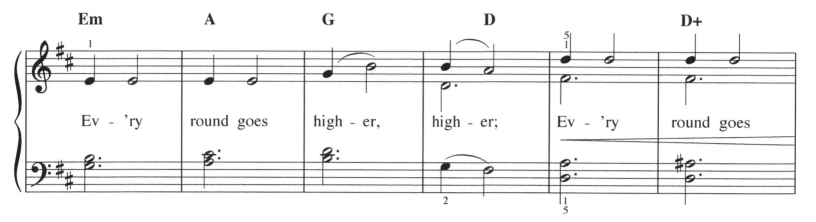

Ev - 'ry round goes high - er, high - er; Ev - 'ry round goes

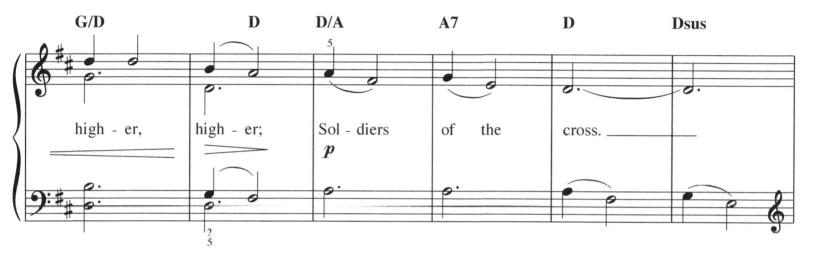

high - er, high - er; Sol - diers of the cross. ____

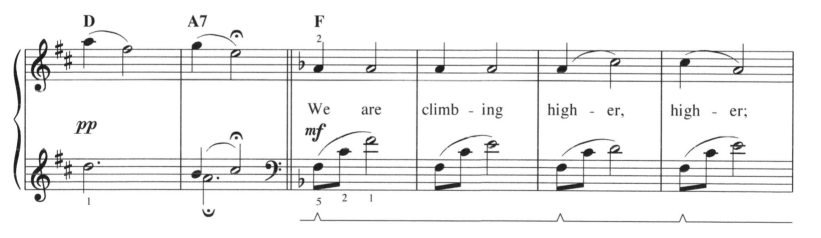

We are climb - ing high - er, high - er;

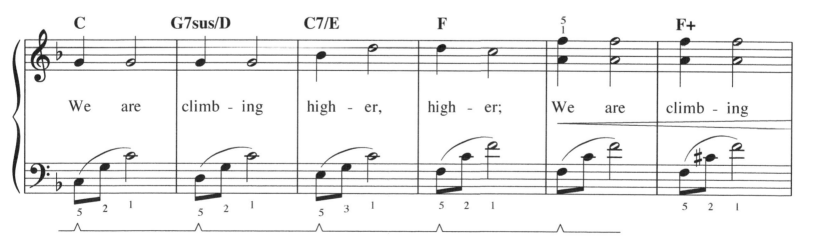

We are climb - ing high - er, high - er; We are climb - ing

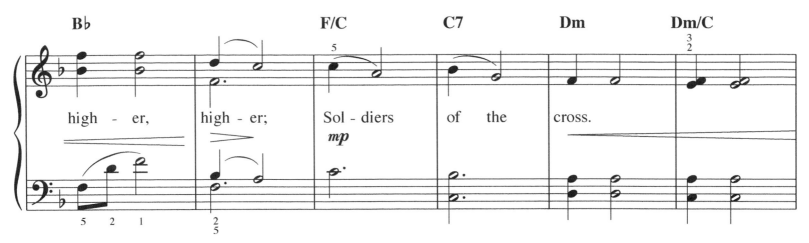

Bb **F/C** **C7** **Dm** **Dm/C**

high - er, high - er; Sol - diers of the cross.

mp

A little slower

Bb **Asus** **A** **D**

If you love Him, why not serve Him?

f

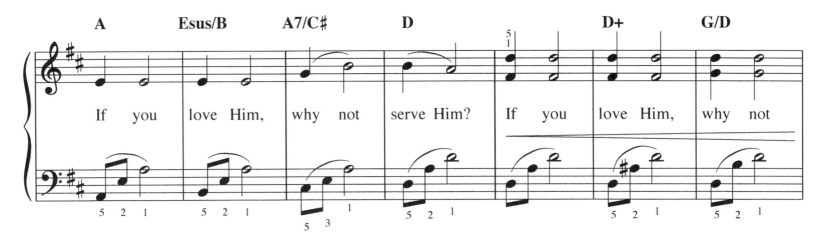

A **Esus/B** **A7/C#** **D** **D+** **G/D**

If you love Him, why not serve Him? If you love Him, why not

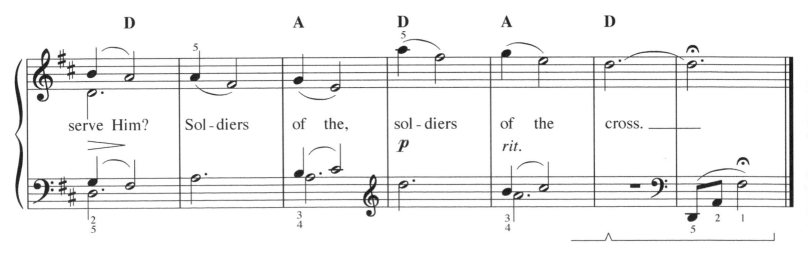

D **A** **D** **A** **D**

serve Him? Sol - diers of the, sol - diers of the cross.

p *rit.*